BLOT OUT THE LAW?

JOE CREWS

Chapter One
The Authority of God's Law

The devil, through sin, has just about wrecked this world of ours. We live in an age of rebellion against all restraint and law. Our nation stands aghast at the big-city gang defiance of social order and property rights, including the right to live. Murder, robbery, and personal assaults have become the trademark of both urban and suburban 20th-century life.

Each day as we read the newspaper it seems that the quality of life has edged downward a little bit further. At times we are tempted to believe that things can get no worse, and that conditions have hit rock bottom. Yet, the next day, even more violent, bizarre crimes are reported, and we simply shake our heads in disbelief. It is difficult to comprehend how a nation like America with its rich Christian heritage could ever depart so far from its founding principles. Even the non-Christian countries are not plagued with as much crime and overall violence as this so-called Christian nation. More crime is reported in Washington, D.C., in 24 hours than Moscow reports in a full year. No doubt the reporting methods are not the same, but it still presents an alarming picture.

The problem becomes more serious when we realize that lawlessness also reaches into the area of religion and affects millions who would never think of killing or raping. It is probable that the great majority of church members in America today carry few convictions against breaking at least one of the Ten Commandments. A very insidious doctrine has been developed in both Catholic and Protestant theology, which has tended to minimize the authority of God's great moral law. It has led many to look lightly upon transgression and has made sin to appear unobjectionable. In fact, sin has lost its horror for multitudes and has become an acceptable mode of life for both youth and adults. Witness the current trends in lifestyle that support this view.

How many young men and women are living together without benefit of marriage! Yet they do not believe such living arrangements should be designated as sin. A large portion of shoplifters are professing Christians, and most of those who belong to churches believe that there is no sin whatsoever involved in violating the seventh-day Sabbath of the fourth commandment.

How can we explain this paradoxical situation among those who profess such high regard for the Bible, and such love for Christ? This question becomes more significant when we consider the historical position of Christianity toward the Ten-Commandment law. Almost all of the great denominations have officially placed themselves on record as supporting the authority of that law. Yet very subtle errors of interpretation have crept into the modern church, leading to the present state of confused loyalty toward the Ten Commandments. How earnestly we need to look at that law and study its relation to God's grace and to salvation itself. It is so easy to accept the popular clichés concerning law and grace without searching out the biblical facts by which we will finally be judged. We must find authoritative scriptural answers to questions like these: In what sense are Christians free from the law? What does it mean to be under the law? Does God's grace nullify the Ten Commandments? Is a Christian justified in breaking any of the Ten Commandments because he is under grace? These are the questions we shall address ourselves to in this important study.

Chapter Two
Condemned to Die

Let us push aside the rubbish of confusion that has obscured the truth about how men are saved. Multitudes have heard emotional discourses on sin and salvation, but they still do not understand the logic and reason that require a blood sacrifice.

Can you imagine the horror of standing before a judge and hearing the sentence of death pronounced against you? Probably not. But you have felt the driving guilt and fear when God's Word stabs you with this sentence: "The wages of sin is death" (Romans 6:23). Why fear and guilt? Because "all have sinned, and come short of the glory of God" (Romans 3:23).

The words are there and the meaning cannot be mistaken. The word "all" might just as well be spelled John Smith or Mary Jones or whatever your name happens to be. The shocking fact is that you are under the sentence of death! You have been found guilty before the law, and there is no court of appeal in the world that can reverse the sentence and find you not guilty. The fact is that you are guilty, just as guilty as sin. According to 1 John 3:4, "sin is the transgression of the law," and you must plead guilty to breaking the law. Whose law did you break? Paul answers quickly, "I had not known sin, but by the law: for I had not known lust, except the law had said, Thou shalt not covet" (Romans 7:7). There it is! The great Ten-Commandment law is the one that was broken, and it demands death for the transgressor.

In desperation the sinner searches for a way to be justified in the sight of that broken law. How can the sentence of death be turned aside? Can man atone for his sins by obeying the commandments of God for the rest of his life? Back comes the answer in language that no one can misinterpret: "Therefore by the deeds of the law there shall no flesh be justified in his sight" (Romans 3:20).

Listen; there is a reason why works will not justify a soul. If a man is found guilty of stealing and is sentenced to ten years in jail, he may indeed justify himself by works. By serving the time of his sentence, the man may satisfy the claims of the law. He is considered perfectly justified and innocent because he has worked out his deliverance by fulfilling the sentence. In the same manner, a murderer may be justified by works if he serves the fifty years of his sentence. But suppose the sentence is death instead of fifty years? Can the prisoner then justify himself by works? Never! Even if he should work for one hundred years at hard labor, the law would still demand death. The truth is that "without shedding of blood is no remission. … So Christ was once offered to bear the sins of many" (Hebrews 9:22–28).

This is why works can never save the sinner. The penalty for sin is not ten years in prison or fifty years at hard labor. The sentence is death, and the law cannot be satisfied except by the shedding of blood. That unchangeable law with its unrelenting death sentence could no more be removed than the throne of God could be toppled. The guilt of the past cannot be erased by resolutions of good behavior in the future. The sinner finally is forced to confess that he owes something that he cannot pay. The law demands death and he cannot satisfy it without forfeiting his own life for eternity.

CHAPTER THREE
THE LAW STILL BINDING

Now we are brought to the question that has created confusion for multitudes of Christians: If the works of the law cannot save a person, is it therefore necessary to keep the law? Apparently this was a burning issue in the early church, because Paul asked the same question in Romans 6:1. "Shall we continue in sin, that grace may abound?" In other words, does grace give us a license to disobey the law of God? His answer is: "God forbid. How shall we, that are dead to sin, live any longer therein?" (verse 2).

How interesting it is that Christians in this age of relativism can invent their own definitions that condone lawbreaking. The Bible says sin is violating the Ten Commandments—the law which has been described as irrelevant and old-fashioned by many modern theologians. Don't be deceived. Every one of those great moral precepts is just as timely and needful today as they were when God wrote them on the imperishable tables of stone. And nothing has ever happened to make them less binding than they were when God gave them. In fact, we are going to discover that Jesus came to magnify the law and to open up its spiritual application, making it more comprehensive than the legalistic Pharisees ever imagined.

Under the distilling influence of Christ's perfect life of obedience, we can see the spiritual details of law-keeping which are neither recognized nor made possible apart from Him.

CHAPTER FOUR
GOD'S LAW—A MIRROR

At this point we must be very careful to designate also what the law cannot do. Even though it points out sin, it has no power to save from sin. There is no justifying, cleansing grace in it. All the works of all the laws would not be sufficient to save a single soul. Why? For the simple reason that we are saved by grace through faith, as a free gift. "Therefore by the deeds of the law there shall no flesh be justified in his sight: for by the law is the knowledge of sin" (Romans 3:20).

Do not stumble over this crucial point. We cannot earn forgiveness by working hard to obey. No sinner can gain favor and acceptance with God because he keeps the law. The law was not made for the purpose of saving or justifying. It was made to show us our need of cleansing and to point us to the great source of cleansing, Jesus Christ, our Lord. The Bible speaks of the law as a mirror to show us what kind of persons we really are. "For if any be a hearer of the word, and not a doer, he is like unto a man beholding his natural face in a glass: For he beholdeth himself, and goeth his way, and straightway forgetteth what manner of man he was. But whoso looketh into the perfect law of liberty, and continueth therein, he being not a forgetful hearer, but a doer of the work, this man shall be blessed in his deed" (James 1:23–25).

It is obvious to all that a mirror cannot remove a spot from the face. Looking into the mirror all day, and even rubbing it over the face, will not provide any cleansing. Its work is to reveal the spot and to point the dirty one to the sink for actual cleansing. The law, in like manner, can only condemn the sinner by giving him knowledge of his condition and then pointing him to the cross for true cleansing. "For by grace are ye saved through faith; and that not of yourselves: it is the gift of God: Not of works, lest any man should boast" (Ephesians 2:8, 9). Paul further emphasizes this point in Galatians 2:16: "Knowing that a man is not justified by the works of the law, but by the faith of Jesus Christ ... for by the works of the law shall no flesh be justified."

Right here we must consider one of the most fallacious propositions ever set forth relating to the law. Countless sincere Christians have accepted the idea that the Old Testament encompasses the dispensation of works and that the New Testament provides for a dispensation of grace. Under this garbled plan people were saved by works in the Old Testament and by grace in the New Testament. This is simply not true. The Bible holds forth only one beautiful, perfect plan for anybody to be saved, and that is by grace through faith. Heaven will not be divided between those who got there by works and those who got there by faith. Every single soul among the redeemed will be a sinner saved by grace.

Those who entered into salvation in the Old Testament were those who trusted the merits of the blood of Jesus Christ, and they demonstrated their faith by bringing a lamb and slaying it. They looked forward in faith to the atoning death of Jesus. We look back in faith to the same death and are saved in exactly the same way. Be very certain that the entire redeemed host throughout eternity will be singing the same song of deliverance, exalting the Lamb slain from the foundations of the world.

CHAPTER FIVE
THE "NEW" LAW OF CHRIST

Some try to dispose of the Ten Commandments on the basis of the "new" commandments of love that Christ introduced. It is certainly true that Jesus laid down two great laws of love as a summary of all the law, but did He give the idea that these were new in point of time? The fact is that He was quoting directly from the Old Testament when He gave those new commandments. "And thou shalt love the LORD thy God with all thine heart, and with all thy soul, and with all thy might" (Deuteronomy 6:5). "Thou shalt love thy neighbour as thyself" (Leviticus 19:18). Certainly, those penetrating spiritual principles had been forgotten by the legalists of Christ's day, and they were new to them in relation to their life and practice. But they were not intended by Jesus to take the place of the Ten Commandments.

When the lawyer asked Jesus which was the greatest commandment in the law, he received the answer: "Thou shalt love the Lord thy God with all thy heart, and with all thy soul, and with all thy mind. This is the first and great commandment. And the second is like unto it, Thou shalt love thy neighbour as thyself. On these two commandments hang all the law and the prophets" (Matthew 22:37–40).

Notice that these two love commandments simply summed up "all the law and the prophets." They all hang upon these two principles of love. Christ was saying that love is the fulfilling of the law just as Paul repeated it later in Romans 13:10. If one loves Christ supremely with heart, soul, and mind, he will obey the first four commandments that have to do with our duty to God. He will not take God's name in vain, worship other gods, etc. If one loves his neighbor as himself, he will obey the last six commandments that relate to our duty to our fellow men. He will not be able to steal from his neighbor, lie about him, etc. Love will lead to obeying or fulfilling all the law.

Chapter Six
Not Under the Law

Often we hear this argument in an effort to belittle the law of God: "Well, since we are not under the law but under grace, we do not need to keep the Ten Commandments any longer." Is this a valid point? The Bible certainly does say that we are not under the law, but does that imply that we are free from the obligation to obey it? The text is found in Romans 6:14, 15.

"For sin shall not have dominion over you: for ye are not under the law, but under grace. What then? shall we sin, because we are not under the law, but under grace? God forbid."

How easily we could prevent confusion if we accepted exactly what the Bible says. Paul gives his own explanation of his statement. After stating that we are not under the law but under grace, he asks, "What then?" This simply means, "How are we to understand this?" Then notice his answer. In anticipation that some will construe his words to mean that you can break the law because you are under grace, he says, "Shall we sin (break the law) because we are not under the law but under grace? God forbid." In the strongest possible language Paul states that being under grace does not give a license to break the law. Yet this is exactly what millions believe today, and they totally ignore Paul's specific warning.

If being under grace does not exempt us from keeping the law, then what does Paul mean by saying that Christians are not under the law? He gives that answer in Romans 3:19. "Now we know that what things soever the law saith, it saith to them who are under the law: that every mouth may be stopped, and all the world may become guilty before God." Here Paul equates being under the law with "being guilty before God." In other words, those who are under the law are guilty of breaking it and are under the condemnation of it. This is why Christians are not under it. They are not breaking it—not guilty and condemned by it. Therefore, they are not under it, but are under the power of grace instead. Later in his argument, Paul points out that the power of grace is greater than the power of sin. This is why he states so emphatically, "For sin shall not have dominion over you: for ye are not under the law, but under grace." Grace overrules the authority of sin, giving power to obey God's law. This is the effective reason that we are not under the law's guilt and condemnation and also why Paul states that we will not continue to sin.

Suppose a murderer has been sentenced to death in the electric chair. Waiting for the execution the man would truly be under the law in every sense of the word—under the guilt, under the condemnation, under the sentence of death, etc. Just before the execution date the governor reviews the condemned man's case and decides to pardon him. In the light of extenuating circumstances the governor exercises his prerogative and sends a full pardon to the prisoner. Now he is no longer under the law but under grace. The law no longer condemns him. He is considered totally justified as far as the charges of the law are concerned. He is free to walk out of the prison and no policeman can lay hands upon him. But now that he is under grace and no longer under the law, can we say that he is free to break the law? Indeed not! In fact, that pardoned man will be doubly obligated to obey the law *because he has found grace* from the governor. In gratitude and love he will be very careful to honor the law of that state which granted him grace. Is that what the Bible says about pardoned sinners? "Do we then make void the law through faith? God forbid: yea, we establish the law" (Romans 3:31). Here is the most explicit answer to the entire problem. Paul asks if the law is nullified for us just because we have had faith in Christ's saving grace. His answer is that the law is established and reinforced in the life of a grace-saved Christian.

The truth of this is so simple and obvious that it should require no repetition, but the devious reasoning of those who try to avoid obedience makes it necessary to press this point a bit further. Have you ever been stopped by a policeman for exceeding the speed limit? It is an embarrassing experience, especially if you know you are guilty. But suppose you really were hurrying to meet a valid emergency, and you pour out your convincing explanation to the policeman as he writes your ticket. Slowly he folds the ticket and tears it up. Then he says, "All right, I'm going to pardon you this time, but …" Now what do you think he means by that word "but"? Surely he means, "but I don't want to ever catch you speeding again." Does this pardon (grace) open the way for you to disobey the law? On the contrary, it adds compelling urgency to your decision not to disobey the law again. Why, then, should any true Christian try to rationalize his way out of obeying the law of God? "If ye love me," Jesus said, "keep my commandments" (John 14:15).

CHAPTER SEVEN
OBEDIENCE—THE TEST OF LOVE

Someone may bring up the objection that after the law has accomplished its purpose of pointing the sinner to Christ for cleansing, it will no longer be needed in the experience of the believer. Is that true? No, indeed. The Christian will always need the watchdog of the law to reveal any deviation from the true path and to point him back to the cleansing cross of Jesus. There will never be a time when that mirror of correction will not be needed in the progressive growth experience of the Christian.

Law and grace do not work in competition with each other but in perfect cooperation. The law points out sin, and grace saves from sin. The law is the will of

God, and grace is the power to do the will of God. We do not obey the law *in order* to be saved but *because* we are saved. A beautiful text which combines the two in their true relationship is Revelation 14:12. "Here is the patience of the saints: here are they that keep the commandments of God, and the faith of Jesus." What a perfect description of faith and works! And the combination is found in those who are "saints."

The works of obedience are the real test of love. This is why they are so necessary in the experience of a true believer. "Faith without works is dead" (James 2:20). No man ever won a fair maiden's heart by words alone. Had there been no flowers, no acts of devotion, no gifts of love, most men would still be searching for a companion. Jesus said, "Not every one that saith unto me, Lord, Lord, shall enter into the kingdom of heaven; but he that doeth the will of my Father which is in heaven" (Matthew 7:21).

Words and profession are not enough. The true evidence is obedience. Today's bumper stickers reflect a shallow concept of love. They say, "Smile if you love Jesus,"

"Honk if you love Jesus"; but what did the Master Himself say? He said, "If ye love me, keep my commandments" (John 14:15). And that is exactly what most people don't want to do. If love makes no demands beyond a smile or wave, then it is welcome; but if the lifestyle must be disturbed, the majority will reject it. Unfortunately, most people today are not looking for truth. They are looking for a smooth, easy, comfortable religion that will allow them to live the way they please and still give assurance of salvation. There is indeed no true religion that can do that for them.

One of the strongest texts in the Bible on this subject is found in 1 John 2:4. "He that saith, I know him, and keepeth not his commandments, is a liar, and the truth is not in him." John could write that with such assurance because it is one of the most deeply established truths in the Bible. Jesus spoke of those who said, "Lord, Lord," but did not do the will of the Father. Then He described many who would seek entrance to the kingdom claiming to be workers of miracles in the name of Christ. But He would sorrowfully have to say, "I never knew you: depart from me" (Matthew 7:21–23). You see, to know Christ is to love Him, and to love Him is to obey Him. The valid assumption of the Bible writers is very clear and simple: If one is not obeying Christ, he does not love Christ. And if he doesn't love the Master, then he doesn't know Him. John assured us, "And this is life eternal, that they might know thee the only true God, and Jesus Christ, whom thou hast sent" (John 17:3). Thus, we can see how knowing and loving and obeying are all tied closely together and are absolutely inseparable in the life of God's faithful people. The beloved John summed it up in these words: "For this is the love of God, that we keep his commandments: and his commandments are not grievous" (1 John 5:3).

CHAPTER EIGHT
IS IT POSSIBLE TO OBEY THE LAW?

Countless Christians have been taught that since the law is spiritual and we are carnal, no human being will ever be able in this life to meet the requirements of the perfect law. Is this true? Has it been given by God as a great idealistic, impossible goal toward which converted souls should struggle but never expect to attain? Is there some hidden reservation or secret meaning in the many commands to obey the ten great rules God wrote on stone? Did God mean what He said and say what He meant?

Many believe that only Christ could have obeyed that law and only because He had special powers that have not been made available to us. Certainly it is true that Jesus is the only One who lived without committing a single act of disobedience. His reason for living that perfect, victorious life is laid out in Romans 8:3, 4: "For what the law could not do, in that it was weak through the flesh, God sending his own Son in the likeness of sinful flesh, and for sin, condemned sin in the flesh: That the righteousness of the law might be fulfilled in us, who walk not after the flesh but after the Spirit."

Do not miss the point that Jesus came to condemn sin by His perfect life in the flesh in order that "the righteousness of the law" might be fulfilled in us. What is that righteousness? The Greek word *dikaima* is used here, which means, literally, "the just requirement" of the law. This can only mean that Christ won His perfect victory in order to make the same victory available to us. Having conquered the devil, showing that in the flesh the law can be obeyed, Christ now offers to come into our hearts and share the victory with us. Only by His strength and indwelling power can the requirements of the law be fulfilled by anyone. Paul said, "I can do all things through Christ which strengtheneth me" (Philippians 4:13).

Not one soul can ever keep one of those Ten Commandments in human power alone, but all of them may be kept through the enabling strength of Jesus. He imputes His righteousness for cleansing and imparts His righteousness for victorious living. Christ came in a body of flesh like our own and depended wholly upon His Father in living His life to demonstrate the kind of victory which is possible for every soul who will likewise draw upon the Father's grace.

Chapter Nine
Judged by the Law

Now, a final question about the subject of the law: How many of the Ten Commandments does one have to break in order to be guilty of sin? James says, "For whosoever shall keep the whole law, and yet offend in one point, he is guilty of all. For he that said, Do not commit adultery, said also, Do not kill. Now if thou commit no adultery, yet if thou kill, thou art become a transgressor of the law. So speak ye, and so do, as they that shall be judged by the law of liberty" (James 2:10–12).

Every individual will be judged at last by the mighty moral code of God's law. To break one is to be guilty of sin. The Bible indicates that the Ten Commandments are like a chain with ten links. When one link is broken, the chain is broken. So it is with the law. Those who stand in the judgment will have to meet the acid test of the Ten Commandments. If a practicing thief should seek entrance into the kingdom, he would be rejected. This is why Paul says thieves will not inherit the heavenly city. Furthermore, the Bible specifically declares that liars, adulterers, idolaters, and covetous men will not be in the kingdom. Why? Because the Ten Commandments forbid those things, and men will be judged finally by that law. Not one person will be admitted into heaven who is willfully violating any one of the Ten Commandments, because breaking one is breaking all.

Someone might object that this is making works the basis of entering the kingdom. No. It is really making love the qualifying factor. Jesus said that the greatest commandment of all is to love God supremely. He also said, "If ye love me, keep my commandments" (John 14:15). Those who practice any known sin are really confessing that they do not love God with all their heart, soul, and mind. So it is the lack of love that shuts them out—not the act of disobedience that exposes that lack. Only when love is motivating the obedience does it become acceptable to

God. Any other work is man's vain attempt to earn salvation and to deny the efficacy of Christ's atoning sacrifice.

CHAPTER TEN
RANSOMED FOR WHAT?

A dramatic illustration of the law-grace doctrine is seen in the story of the slave auctions in old New Orleans long ago. Two planters were bidding for an old Negro slave who kept shouting his rebellion from the auction block. Finally, one of the planters won the bid and took the slave in his wagon back to the farm. Throughout the journey the defiant black man declared that he would not work for the new owner. When they arrived at the plantation, the planter dropped the shackles from the newly bought slave and said, "You are free to go. You are no longer a slave. I bought you in order to give you your liberty."

According to the story, the old man fell at the feet of the planter and said, "Master, I'll serve you forever."

In like manner, we were all held in the bondage of sin, condemnation, and death. Christ then paid the price to secure our freedom from that hopeless slavery. Lovingly He tells us that the reason He made the sacrifice was to set us free. What should our response be? Every ransomed child of God should fall at His feet and say, "Master, I love you for what you did for me. I'll serve you the rest of my life."

Think it through for a moment. Jesus had to die because the law had been broken. Sin demanded death. If the law could have been abrogated, the penalty of sin would have been set aside also. "For where no law is, there is no transgression" (Romans 4:15). So strong was the authority of that unchangeable law that God Himself could not abolish it—not even to save His own Son from death.

The old, old story of the two brothers is almost a perfect illustration of both law and grace in operation. The older brother was a judge. His younger brother was brought before him as a transgressor of the law. From all the evidence it was clear to all that he was guilty. The court was tense. Would the judge mete out justice in such a case? The judge looked at his brother and sternly declared him guilty. Then he stunned the court by imposing the maximum fine. But immediately he left the bench and threw his arms around his brother and said, "I had to do it because you are guilty. I know you cannot pay the fine, but I will pay it for you."

The point of the story is dramatic in its impact. The brother was forgiven, but the penalty was not. It had to be paid. But by paying the maximum penalty, the judge not only did not abolish the law, but he greatly magnified it. He demonstrated that its binding claims could never be voided. In the same sense, God would not and could not abolish the law to save His beloved Son. It cost something to uphold the law and pay the maximum penalty. No one will ever know how much it cost the Son of God. But how thankful we should be that His love was as perfect as His justice. In His own body He bore the penalty, satisfied the law, and justified the transgressor.

Can't you see that no greater demonstration could have been made to prove the permanence of the Ten Commandments? In the entire universe God could not have displayed a more convincing and irrefutable argument in favor of His law. Yet, in the face of this tremendous exhibition, misguided millions of poor, feeble men belittle the government of God by belittling His law. They seem not to understand that the law is only a reflection of His holiness and righteousness. To speak of its abolition is to border on treason against the divine government of heaven.

Look into that holy law right now for a divine revelation of what God wants your life to be. Confess that you have no strength to live up to that perfect standard. Then turn your eyes to the only One who has kept that law perfectly and who desires this very moment to enter your life with enabling power. He will fulfill the righteousness of the law—the just requirements of the law—in you, so that you can say with Paul, "Christ liveth in me: and the life which I now live in the flesh I live by the faith of the Son of God, who loved me, and gave himself for me" (Galatians 2:20).